"Reading Marilyn McVicker's poetry has touched me in many ways. She teaches us all how to live life as authentic, fully-alive, compassionate human beings. As a musician and poet, her book *As for Life* is a composition of her chronic illness written in four movements in which she writes the score of her pain, and her love of life. Her poems may seem harsh in their honesty but they are not without mercy; rather, they're shared experiences and insights that not only help us to be better friends, family and physicians to those with chronic illness, but may save us when we are someday faced with our own agonies...I am humbled by the lessons I found in Marilyn's poetry."—**Jade Pierce, B.S., M.Ac.Licensed acupuncturist and practitioner of Traditional Asian Medicine**

Advance Praise: *As for Life*

"To every prospective reader of *As for Life* I would say, 'Brace yourself. Do not avert your gaze. Here you will experience revelation that will increase your understanding.' Marilyn McVicker does not countenance equivocation in herself or in others. This may well be the most candid volume of poetry I ever read. Be prepared."
—Fred Chappell, N.C. Poet Laureate, 1997-2002

"Even in illness there is life and love, Marilyn McVicker proclaims in *As for Life*, her memoir of poems introducing us to her life with primary immune deficiency. McVicker opens us to the rage and grief, joy and beauty of a life confined to a remote mountain cove in Western North Carolina. I am strengthened, humbled, and inspired by her elegant and honest poems—a resilient life celebrated in poetry."
—Jennie Boyd Bull, *Learning to Weave: A Woman-Loving Life*, **volunteer with My Neighbors, eldercare network**

"Marilyn McVicker takes us on a journey of the isolation experienced due to chronic illness. The use of poetic story telling is relatable and brings the reader to experience how, after a full day of pushing one's self through the necessary tasks, and when evening comes, the body relaxes and all the pain comes at the time when rest is expected…The author takes the reader on a journey of chronic illness and how it defines the challenges of the simplest tasks that are often never considered as we move through the normal activities of each day. Poetically orchestrated, the complications of wanting to be normal and the body saying otherwise, strands through each poem…" **–Patricia Mayorga, Judge, North Carolina Poetry Society's 2020 Lena Shull Book Award, Editor-in-Chief,** *Poets' Espresso Review.*

"The varied cadences and stunning word choices in *As for Life*, lead the reader to understand the myriad daily tasks and fluctuating emotions that come with a rare, chronic illness. McVicker asks us to, 'Consider this body. So much, for so long. Not enough, for too long./ So much pain and loss. Joys and hopes filled and dashed./ Life and death, handled simultaneously.' Living a life of isolation, she gazes out her many windows to find comfort and hope in nature and thinks of 'the small joys' that sustain her."**—Kathy Weisfeld, Chair, Carolina Mountains Literary Festival, Poet**

"*As for Life* is a catharsis of raw emotion, a reflection of one person's life and loss while enduring chronic illness. Very enlightening! A must-read for health care professionals and medical/nursing students interested in the provision of patient-centered care." **—Laura H. Young, MSN, DNP, AGNP-C Compassionate Care of WNC, Palliative Care**

A S
F O R
L I F E

A memoir in poetry
exploring the isolation & loss
of chronic illness

Marilyn McVicker

REDHAWK
PUBLICATIONS

Redhawk Publications
The Catawba Valley Community College Press
2550 US Hwy 70 SE
Hickory NC 28602

ISBN: 978-1-952485-70-1

Library of Congress Number: 2022936567

Printed in the United States of America

redhawkpublications.com

Cover Design: Erin Louise Talbert
Author Photo: Ellen E. Kinnear

Dedication

To Ellen, the most fiercely determined and steadfast person I know.
Thank you for sharing a life and an illness with me.

To cortisone, immune globulin, and antibiotics, without which
I would not be alive.

To my body, for surviving.

To those living with chronic illness.
May you find friends who listen, understand and support.

As for Life

"I will tell you not what you want to hear
but what I know will be true because I have lived it."

Arthur W. Frank
The Wounded Storyteller

~~~

"Whatever I wrote, I wrote out of that pain,
and whatever I wrote assuaged the pain a little
but never enough."

Nancy Mairs
Ordinary Time

~~~

"Things happened that we did not want, things that were painful
and disruptive. But they brought unexpected opportunities once
they happened, and there was no way of turning back. In order to
see the opportunities, though, you must accept what happened as if
you have chosen it."

Arnold R. Beisser
Flying Without Wings; Personal Reflections on Being Disabled

Acknowledgments

I gratefully acknowledge:

The editors of the publications where the following poems are forthcoming, or have previously appeared:

Breath & Shadow: "Sometimes in the Evening"

Expressions: Literature and Art by People with Disabilities: "It Hurts"

Front Porch Review: "Complicated Grief Never Ends," "Volley of Darkness"

Gateways: The Creative Arts Journal of Mitchell, Avery and Yancey Counties: "Double Crochet," "How Are You Doing?"

Kaleidoscope: "How I Have Been Touched"

The Healing Muse: "Doctors"

Red Clay Review: "Pain," "Silence," "Snowed In"

Redheaded Stepchild: "As for Life"

Wordgathering: "Hair Loss," "No Technological Devices Will Assist"

Acknowledgments, continued

Malaprop's Bookstore for awarding semi-finalist to the poem, "Oranges in Snow" in their Poem-in-a-Pocket Contest.

North Carolina Poetry Society, for awarding an Honorable Mention to this manuscript in their 2020 Lena Shull Book Contest.

My wife, who inspired, listened, edited, and set aside time to support my poetry; my three loving daughters; my monthly poetry group; grandparents who believed in my writing; Pat Riviere-Seel and Richard Chess, for their compassionate mentorship; countless doctors and health professionals who listened and assisted, and those health professionals who were unable to assist, but served to help develop my courage and voice; and to all those countless others living in isolation, or with chronic illness and disability. Thank you.

Table of Contents

Foreword

I hadn't expected to be caught breathless at points by Marilyn's expression. I couldn't have guessed part of me would initially rush through the reading, as if more quickly skimming its surfaces could spare me the empathetic suffering, Marilyn's conveyance being that poignant. I should have guessed that the ways of getting to know and understand Marilyn could continue so dramatically to deepen and unfold, like exploring cave systems, then a passage suddenly branches and tunnels surprisingly deeper into even more territory worthy of wonder.

In *As for Life*, her memoir in poetry, we get not only Marilyn's powerful, empowering, enlightening, and sometimes shocking understanding of long-term chronic illness's realities. With it, we also get the privilege of holding the other end of what may be her lifeline—these poems—wherein she's choosing us, inviting us in, sometimes when there has been no one else, and disclosing intimacies heretofore confined to her isolation. We get the honor to be audience to her saving her own life.

I first met Marilyn some years back, at a community gathering of writers. New, I hadn't understood the breach when, well intentioned, I'd slid my seat closer to bridge the gap between the group and this woman set off by herself. Nor could I have understood then what it may have taken for her to be able to attend this rare gathering and what a coup being there may have involved. More recently, I've had the honor of getting to know Marilyn through our local Death Seeding Life collective and my private healing practice. It's felt like a hallowed way of getting to know someone—her—walking beside them when they "[d]on't fit in to the Land/ of the Living, or the Land of the Dying," and as they're courageously resolving their unfinished business between.

An aspect I especially appreciate about Marilyn's self-expression, this collection no exception, is its embrace of what I've heard called wholeness. By this, I mean that particular aspects—be they isolation, pain, rage, grief, despair—are not necessarily dualized as "bad" or "wrong," but are instead, simply real parts of the totality, granted their deserving seat at the table among their kin of understanding, courage, power, praise, and grace. I suppose it's from this larger perspective we get, for example, in "This is a Poem about Illness," what seems the collection's title track, images of "nausea that rolls in like a sea surge," "mind-splitting headaches," "foreign mitochondria multiplying in my lymph glands," "my body once again/ under siege" and "four subcutaneous needles in my abdomen,/ the third day this week" as a prelude to "learning to forgive my own body," "to let go of so much," "to open my heart and hear" even what sometimes feels cruel, "to remain forgiving and up-beat" amid being misunderstood, and "to be grateful for/ small things [and] small kindnesses," all the more prized for their rarity. We hear how "others cannot comprehend/ how I can enjoy a rich and full spiritual life" while "suffering from a genetic illness." And we bear witness, its final stanza, to the juxtaposition of "knowing/ I am fully alive, singing, 'Hallelujah,'/ through my ever-present tears." I savor this co-mingling and playing of contrasts, often within one poem, the whole way through the collection: in "Sometimes," "The Body," "Hope," "Double Crochet," "Complicated Grief Never Ends," "What Matters"...I could keep going, but you'll see for yourself.

For those who, like Marilyn, endure "the kind of illness that is invisible" and whose "resolution...never comes," you especially may prize about this collection, hearing one's own marginalized, secret experience that "no one sees/ or hears" so accurately, artfully articulated into recognition that you can't help but exclaim the triumph and tragedy of "Yes! YES! That's IT!" every other page. You may recognize in these poems the isolation despite even a loving spouse or attentive children, the grief of what could have been but never will be, the relentless pain and medical regimen, the illness-beyond-cancer that our society has no understanding of or patience for, and the equal desires for the "intent [for] surviving as long as I can" and the relief "to say goodbye [and] know/ the suffering will be over." You may celebrate Marilyn's audacity to speak aloud what you have so often thought but never been able to say: in "To My Friend with Cancer," "I Called to Ask You a Question," "To my Friend at the Beach" and most empowering, "Things People Say." You may find comfort in the bottom line realizations she offers after "Countless nights/ Of utter despair": "gratitude/ [for] the warm house.../Brain That still works Heart Still open Soul/ Which still hopes And wants" and "that Even with illness And isolation My one life/ Matters." You may experience aspects of your own life— maybe some not before realized—reflected back to you with insight and understanding.

For those who stand on the other side of this great divide—like me, for now—Marilyn offers us gentle instruction in these poems. She uses second person to invite us into her experience: "Your world crashes, shrinks/ to the warmth of your coverlet." And to model what she'd wish for, so we may make more skillful choices: "You imagine a friend coming to visit, a friend/ who would know to wear a mask, sit at a distance,/ talk slowly, softly listen, limit their time, not wear you out." She uses commands and repetition to help us develop our perspective by virtue of hers: "Celebrate the body that stands when you bid... Celebrate the body that breathes without wheezes...Celebrate the senses, which pleasure at the soothe of touch." She continues in that same poem: "Consider love...Something personal said because you/ were a person before being a patient... Then consider the body in illness... Unable/ to be healed, understood, or even accepted... Consider the raw, raked emotion of this sick person... Consider, how little things become so important." She challenges in a different poem: "Imagine if your doctor had said, 'There's not/ much we can do'... Can you even imagine/ what it might feel like to be 'ripped off' by the last/ fifty years of chronic illness? You are in remission./ I am not." We can be the wiser and more compassionate for being invited into her shoes and heeding her requests.

Most significantly, I don't know if I've ever felt so hospitably invited into the intimacy of such painful solitude as I have in these poems. In "Traveling to the Specialist," we are with her even "peeing in buckets at rest stop" since she cannot risk infection in public restrooms. In "The Veil of Silence," she says about her friend Douglas, "I didn't tell him... how I cope." But she tells us. With him she knows to "Keep it/ simple. Keep it light." But with us she reveals the complexities and depths. In "I Watch Her through my Window," we experience the gulf that separates even loving spouse from spouse with chronic illness; yet we experience it from "this [same] side of the window" as Marilyn, as if even closer to her than a spouse in this moment.

As for Life brings together Marilyn's hard-won wisdom from a lifetime of experience with chronic illness and shares it with us. Whether we be chronically ill ourselves, love someone chronically ill, or professionally support those chronically ill, Marilyn's collection will enrich our lives.

—Jennifer Dorfield
Founder, Returning Home Healing
Member, Death Seeding Life Collective

Preface

The world is in the midst of the coronavirus pandemic. We have been quarantined, on lock-down, doing everything possible to avoid contracting this deadly virus. We are at home; the gate to our driveway is shut; we are not leaving to shop or get gasoline; we have seen no one else for months. We do not know how long this period of quarantine and isolation will last.

The wearing of face masks has been mandated by the government. Social isolation practices are encouraged. Groceries and other essential services are still operating, but it is often difficult to procure various household items due to production and shipping delays. Online ordering is troublesome, with many items being unavailable, marked up in price or sold out.

Protecting ourselves from viral disease has been something I have been practicing for a lifetime. Isolation and careful maneuvering in family and public situations are nothing new to me. My primary immune deficiency has been a lifetime challenge. PID (primary immune deficiency) is a rare disease, not generally understood by physicians, and certainly not by the general public. My need to infuse immune globulin, take antibiotics, wash, clean, disinfect, wear a mask in public, and avoid others during flu season, is constant and real. Last year, contracting Flu A left me in critical condition in the ICU for two weeks. Prior to COVID-19, my insistence on meeting people only outdoors, seated at a distance, was difficult to negotiate. My boundaries were pushed at every opportunity. I have been doubted, misunderstood and humiliated by my susceptibility to viral, fungal and bacterial infections.

The poems in this document were, for the most part, written in the years preceding this pandemic. Today, as I finish putting this manuscript together, although the concept of isolation and loss have formed the architecture of my life, I realize that these same considerations are now more pertinent to a greater section of the population, than ever before. I have rewritten this foreword to include the current situation, as it relates to the lives of many healthy people, as well as those who live with chronic illness.

§

I have been sick since I was a child. I was born in 1952. David Vetter, the "Bubble Boy," wasn't born until 1971, after I had been sick for almost twenty years. I was a patient at a leading medical institution, and although my frequent infections were recognized and treated, research into primary immune deficiency was in its nascent stages of recognition and research. My diagnosis of primary immune deficiency was not understood or diagnosed. Appropriate treatment was not started until several decades later.

Meanwhile, through childhood and young adulthood, I suffered long bouts of illness from frequent bacterial and viral infections which interrupted plans, school, summer vacations and holidays. Attendance records reflect frequent absences; I missed 40% of school days. Not knowing any other way of life, I persevered, kept up with my chores and obligations, school work and social calendar. I pushed through and carried on. While my health degenerated, I feverishly propelled myself forward to create a life.

Instead of "growing out of it," as we were told and had hoped, my health became worse. Illness became more frequent and deep-seated. Nevertheless, I went to college, pursued a career, participated in community events and volunteer activities. Later, when I had a family of my own and was actively involved in my profession, interruptions from serious illness carried more ramifications. In my thirties, I was so frequently ill for long periods of time, it became impossible for me to work; I was forced into disability retirement.

As time has progressed, my illness has also progressed. Additional diagnoses have accrued. My losses have increased, along with my isolation and the time spent managing an ever-expanding list of rare medical conditions that necessitate rigorous self-care, and myriad resources.

Over thirty-five years ago, I began to write about my experience with illness. The successive losses of so many creative and fulfilling pursuits, along with the severe risk of infection, limited many of the ways in which I had previously expressed myself. Writing became my principal instrument of articulation and communication, my safety-valve, my salvation.

I read everything I could find on my rare conditions. During those early years, there was not much published about immune deficiency or chronic illness, and certainly not the pervasive illness I was encountering. More recently, writing has appeared responding to AIDS or cancer. But chronic long-term illness, the type with which you don't get better, don't die, and don't go into remission, was not described, or even discussed. The few narrations I have welcomed over the years, where authors were courageous enough to express the complexities of chronic illness, have been an inspiration. Reading that someone else felt as I did, lost what I had lost, and survived, was encouraging. The authors' openness and truth, was its own reward.

In my own compositions I have tried to express the inexpressible, capture the various moods and vicissitudes, the palette of chronic illness with all of its suffering and loss, but also with its moments of transcendence and joy. I have wanted to recount what I ravenously wanted to read. My goal has been to offer what has provided meaning to me: honesty, transparency, authenticity. I wanted to give words to the story of my illness and what I have learned.

Today, in the midst of the pandemic, people are being forced, by social isolation, to adopt practices I have been doing for years. Persons who previously refused to wear masks because they were uncomfortable, hot, or caused their glasses to fog, are now having to wear them for their own protection. There is more understanding as to why I do not invite people indoors, and why, I only see others at a safe distance, outdoors. The community understands why hugs and handshakes are no longer safe practices. I wonder whether my hairdresser, who refused to wear a mask to protect me prior to COVID-19, is now wearing a mask, herself.

Individuals are using hand sanitizer, cleaning more often, and less likely to think I am phobic because I carry around a container of alcohol wipes, wear gloves, change my clothing after coming into the house, and clean "high touch surface areas" daily. Neighbors and friends are reaching out to assist and support. Others who were previously reluctant to video chat with me, are now requesting this online form of communication, as they experience isolation and loneliness, themselves. Local poetry groups are now uploading poems for regular online sharing, something they didn't consider all the years I was unable to attend, but are now embracing as they, too, encounter the ravages of cancelled opportunities. Doctors are offering telemedicine services, something that was available previously, but rarely used. Classes and meetings are routinely held online.

There is more patience and accommodation for seniors needing guidance with new technology. Stores are offering curb-side pick-up. Even our postal carrier is careful to leave my package in the shed, not traipse onto my porch in his contaminated shoes, and waive his requirement that I use his stylus to log-in package delivery.

I have been isolated since childhood, in one form or another. In the last several years, my need for isolation and protection has increased. I am pleased society is coming to understand, in a personal way, what I have lived with for so long. It is easy to understand my irritation with the frustration of those living with isolation for a mere few months, when I have lived this way most of my life. I hope that when life returns to "normal," these insights and accommodations will not be forgotten or overlooked. It is my wish that the inroads and protections put in place, will remain, just as I would desire that people not disassemble a wheelchair ramp, thinking it unnecessary after the conference.

There are questions and considerations that remain. A vaccine will not work for me because I do not make antibodies. Will there be anything to help me with this new viral threat? Will this virus be quiet during the summer months, and allow me to visit with others without serious risk? Will I be able to travel for medical care? Will my physicians continue telemedicine services?

I must warn the reader that my writing is not intended to be uplifting or inspirational. For every moment or emotion I have captured on paper, there are other experiences, just as strong, but opposite. It has been a balancing act to learn to accept how I feel on any given day, to embrace and express my own humanity. I offer these poems to you, and hope you glean some satisfaction from knowing that even in illness, there is life and love; even with exquisite suffering there is exuberance and abundance.

—Marilyn McVicker

~ ONE ~

Pain

Shrill siren music
Buzzes in head
Building
Pounding
Mounting
The rattle
Of a striking snake
Shaking faster
Accelerando threatens
To explode

Cacophony
Millions of cicadas
Shrieking their litany
Swirling noise
Swarming round my head
Progressing
Chord to chord
Tension building
Submediant
Leading tone
Dominant seventh
Dominant seventh
Dominant seventh
Hanging there
In tension
Waiting for resolution
That never comes

What I Miss

A List Poem

Visiting friends in their homes.
Inviting others into my house.
Being outdoors, anywhere, with friends or family.
Spending holidays with children and grandchildren.
Eating meals cooked by others.
Eating at restaurants.
Going to a concert, movie, or play.
Going anywhere, where there are others.
Meeting new people.
Shopping.
Getting dressed up.
Snuggling with a child.
Petting a dog.
Playing in the symphony.
Performing on my flute.
Standing before an audience.
Diving into a pool.
Swimming seventy-two laps.
Being outdoors on sunny days.
Basking in the sun.
Walking on the beach.
Working on my car.
Digging in the dirt.
Getting up each morning.
Knowing I'll have enough energy
to stay on my feet until bedtime.
Having a day when I'm not in pain.
Being able to move my body smoothly,
bend, twist, sweat and ache.
Believing I will recover.

The Clock on the Wall

with thanks to Gertrude Stein

I have not come to arrive.
If I arrived, I arrived
ever at all.
The ebony clock on the wall
ticks on the end. The day falls,
the day falls, the day all
arrived, arrived without me.

I did not come to arrive.
If I arrived, it was only to survive.
To survive and surmise, surprised,
I derive to do more than survive.
While the minutes tick on, and arrive
one by one, by the clock on the wall,
which arrives, arrives without me.

I did not come to arrive,
but do more than survive.
And come and go, so more than slow.
But there I surmise, while the clock ticks slow,
to do and go, moving to and fro.
So the minutes tick on, so sweet, so low.
They arrive, ticking on, without me.

Doctors

I breathe, review my notes,
while the clock ticks the minutes,
weeks, years of illness, decanted
into a 20-minute appointment.

I have driven so many miles.
Will she listen?
Will she walk in with a smile?

I have had so many doctors wear
their impertinence like stethoscopes.
"Well, you certainly don't look sick."
"Your diagnosis is too complicated."
"There's nothing I can do to help you."

This poem is not for all those pompous,
frenzied physicians.

This poem is for the doctor who pulled
up a chair, made eye contact, listened.
This poem is for the doctor who ventured
from behind the computer, paid attention,
asked intelligent questions.

This poem is for the doctor who did not
reflexively grab the prescription pad,
realized I needed medical care, admitted
he couldn't help, found someone who could.

This poem is for the doctor who worked
to find the right diagnosis, taught me to give
my own injections, started home infusions,
called each week to check in.

This poem is for the doctor who understood
his partnership was more important than healing
that would never come.

How I Have Been Touched

In one week
Twenty-five intravenous needle sticks
Three blood draws
Cold disc of stethoscope
Nurses prep and pressure pulse points

Ministrations to infected shingles
Twice daily ointment
Replacing bandages

Today
The chiropractor
Manipulated my spine
Adjusted my back
Up and down the length
Of my entire body

I felt skin ripple
Muscles relax
Felt all of one piece
A whole person

Not a series
Of broken parts

I cried facedown
On the examination table
Cried at the tenderness
Of one who would merely
Touch

Oranges and Snow

You are chopping oranges
to quench my thirst.

I do bed yoga in the sunroom,
try to stretch this sick and sore body
back into human shape.
The window cracked open,
winter winds rattle
biting breath of snow.

Too tired to move off the floor.

I am grateful
for chopped oranges.
If I were well, we would be out
hiking in the snow,
even now.

The Void

I live my life behind closed windows,
protected inside these four walls.

Outside my window, a neighbor
mows his grass. Inside, I cannot hear.

All I hear is the whisper of the ceiling fan,
hum of the air filters, hiss of my oxygen.

All I feel is pain in my body, grief
in my belly, hopes knotted in my throat.

The anger and despair, sucked up
by the ceiling fan, whirled around,
dispersed into the void.

No Technological Devices Will Assist

No wheelchair ramp, no braces,
no cane, walker or interpreter,
no special van, door knobs,
no thirty-six-inch-wide doors
will serve to give me access.

No accommodation will change the facts.
There's nothing you, or I, medicine or
technology, nothing even love, can do.

Not chemotherapy or radiation, not a pill,
a treatment, not even an infusion of immune
globulin will replace the cellular immunity,
the natural killer cells, the monocytes,
lymphocytes, that are deficient. The primary
immune deficiency that makes human interaction
the most virally-laden, life-threatening experience,
that keeps me infected, isolated, alone, left out,
misunderstood, and ill.

Chronic illness may be invisible. No, I don't
smoke or drink. I'm not obese. I exercise, eat
a healthy diet, take vitamins, am disciplined,
motivated, keep a schedule.

You probably never heard of my disease. It's not
poster worthy. It's genetic. It's become worse.
It's not what I counted on. I haven't become
used to it. And today I'm angry about it.

The Rest of my Life

I don't know what to do
with the rest of my life,
except ache.
Continual aches
swell and throb.
Bones pierce
like glass, flashing
from toe to hip
with each step.
Losses accrue.
More battles, more pain.
Each day's waking,
each night's dreaming.

A timeline of aches
sprawls backwards.
I grieve,
slowly dying
in the dark.
Where no one sees
or hears.

Sometimes in the Evening

Sometimes, in the evening, I get the urge
to go to a poetry slam, share a bucket
of popcorn at the latest movie,
go to the Orange Peel and dance all night.

Sometimes, on a summer evening, I get
the urge to put my hair up, go out for
a root beer float, go down to the harbor,
sip frozen daiquiris, strut my stuff.

Sometimes, when the shadows lengthen
at the end of a long day, I want to see
familiar faces, share a bottle of wine,
good-natured belly laughs, be among
those who love me, be a part of the world,
see, hear, touch, feel, smell and taste.

You would think, after all these years
these urges would fade.

Small Joys

The small joys that sustain me
Wood thrush at dawn   Song of
the katydids   Clouds trailing across
the sky   Wrens nesting on the porch

Meanwhile   Home   Sick   Phone rings
Stove beeps   Microwave dings   Dryer buzzes
Brakes squeal   Truck delivers immune globulin

My five senses   The joys that sustain me
Honed to sharpness   Wind in the pines
Sliver of moon on a dark sky   Smell of my dog
Softness of moss   Hug of a tree
Fire pinks blooming on the hill

Cradled

Outside, the car is lost in snow, the blizzard rages. Trees form a buttress around the house, my cave. A candle glows on the table. Slippers next to the couch witness there is no place to go. Here, rooted to my space, I sink into the enveloping sofa. The storm wages, unleashing winter's wild fury, sending cold blasts. Inside my covers, massive cushions press in, reflect my warmth, cradle me in tenderness. The weight of my languid fever pulls me into padded pillows. Sinking into crevices, I am entombed in softened silence of immense depth.

Validation

I drove home with my lab report.
Just picked it up. No wonder I feel
I could be scraped off the floor.
My cortisol levels are dangerously low.

Why am I so thrilled with these results?
I'm not really happy my levels are low.
I'm not delighted I can barely stay
on the chair. I'm not enchanted
with having to take supplements,
getting fat and moon-faced.

I'm satisfied because it is validating.
It says right here on this lab slip,
there is an explanation, a reason
why I can't stand up, can't think,
can't do much. I am not lazy,
undisciplined, complaining,
or even overdoing it.

I have previous reports:
immune deficiency, low thyroid,
neutropenia, autoimmune disease.
My degenerative arthritis is right there
on the X-ray. There isn't much to do
for any of it—infusions, anti-virals,
antibiotics, follow-up lab reports.

This isn't a passport, a ticket
to a concert, directions to a family
reunion, invitation to dinner with
friends, or even a travel brochure.

Still, I'm pleased with this lab slip.
Just this small piece of paper,
this simple lab slip.

Snowed In

Baltimore is snowed in by a blizzard.
For three days, the entire city
has lived the way I always do.

Activity, ground to a halt, confined
to home, walled in with certain boundaries,
the world outside too treacherous to enter.

Three days have been long enough. The city
is ready to be free of its confinement, eager
to dig itself out. The novelty has worn off.

The snow makes absolutely no difference to me.
From my bed, the storm is only another channel
on my television. It is not even a nuisance.

It is a welcome difference, a momentary
entertainment in the succession of endless days
between these blankets.

I Watch Her through my Window

I watch her from indoors. I cannot read a book
when she is working outside my window. I am
intrigued watching her strong arms dig up the
tiger lilies, lift weighty clumps into the wheelbarrow.
I watch her uproot a dead tree, as if only a peony,
wrestle the giant timber as if it were mere fire wood.

Outside, she lifts the heavy mattock over her head,
poised in mid-air. She pauses, steadies, takes aim,
brings it down, a resounding thud. Her muscles taut,
skin shines bronze. Shorter than I, she is fully grey
at sixty-eight. She is sleeveless, in shorts. Boots
and gloves, her only protective gear.

Indoors, I wear a sweatshirt. The autumn air has a chill.
On this side of the window, I am learning to value
caring for my body and its illness, to be content
appreciating the view, simply watching the woman I love.
I turn from the window, close my book, can barely lift
the laundry basket, as I return to my chores.

Apology

I'm sorry I am sick   Sorry I cannot
go shopping with you   Cannot help
in the yard   Cannot go dancing tonight
Take that hike we planned   Sorry our
vacations are to the clinic   And not
the Outer Banks

I'm sorry I am sick   Sorry my illness
takes up our time   Sorry I cost
so much money   We talk so much
about my illness   That I cause
so much worry

I'm sorry you're sleeping in a chair
Second night at the hospital   While
I'm taking up the only bed in the room

I'm sorry you are old and I am old   And we
have done illness together   For over
thirty years   We could have hiked more trails
Danced more   Gone to the Outer Banks
But we didn't   And you never made me feel bad

Instead we played cards by candlelight
Silver and china at the dining room table
Sang aloud while swinging on the glider
Watched fire flies   Sat by the woodstove
Read poetry aloud   Dug gardens
Planted bushes

We missed seeing grandchildren   Never got
to the Grand Canyon   Didn't boat on Lake Erie
So much we would have done   We could not do

I'm sorry, sorry, sorry   And I love you
Thank you for loving me

Traveling to the Specialist

It's two days of packing to go, making
arrangements for the mail, the cats,
taking all the medications, the food.

It's stopping in large parking lots
to eat our picnic meals inside the car,
because I cannot go in restaurants.

It's peeing in buckets at rest stops, since
I cannot use restrooms. It's staying in
hotels that cannot accommodate me,

or which do make accommodations, with
great fanfare. It's doctors who tell me how rare
my medical condition is, as if I don't already

know. It's looking at their faces, watching
them disengage when they realize
my complications, my age. It's hearing

I don't need their specialty. Knowing I don't
fit in to hospice. Don't fit in to the Land
of the Living, or the Land of the Dying.

It's knowing there isn't any cure, no specialist
smarter than the ones I've seen. Knowing this is
the end of the road. The only way to go, is down.

Immune Globulin Infusion

I wake at six o'clock, walk to the refrigerator,
take out three bottles of gamma globulin, set them
on the counter to come to room temperature.

> Prescribing Physician: Richard Reynolds, MD.

I race through my morning, try to complete all activities
before lunch.

> Primary Diagnosis:
> Combined Immune Deficiency.

After lunch I assemble papers, books, a bowl of cashews,
cold glass of ginger ale, on the overbed table.

> Treatment: Gamunex™ 10%, 7 grams administered
> through four needles placed subcutaneously.
> Portable Graseby™ pump injects gamma globulin
> over seven-hours. Administer every third day.

I walk into my study, turn on the digital photo cube next to
my infusion supplies— Yellow Mountain mullein,
Over-Mountain Victory Trail, Jane Bald bluets blooming,
Carver's Gap spruce flocked in snow.

> Wash hands with antibacterial soap.
> Set up a clean work area.
> Wash surface with antiseptic cleanser.
> Use a clean towel to provide clean field for supplies.

The phone rings. I cannot answer it. I lay supplies on the clean
towel-- bottle of gamma globulin, the four-needle set, four
35-mL syringes, transfer spikes, anaphylaxis kit, alcohol prep pads,
gauze pads, paper tape, IV dressing, thermometer, infusion log.

I wash my hands, return to the table. I remember the infusion
center at the hospital, solicitous nurses bringing warmed blankets,
cold orange juice, friendly smiles, careful concern, attentive interest.

I remove the protective lid from the Gamunex™ vial, wipe the top
with the alcohol pad, use the transfer spike to pierce the latex-free
stopper, invert the vial, slowly, withdraw the medication. I tap
the air bubbles out, attach the needle set, flush the product
through each of the four needles, one at a time, by opening
and closing the clamps.

My dog, Coriander, used to sense my sadness on infusion day.
She would come lay her head on my lap, look up with warm
brown eyes, lie at my feet. She has been dead for six years.

I get up, go to the bathroom, wash my hands again. I come back,
sit down, position myself, and locate four sites—two on my
abdomen, two on my upper thighs. I clean the first site
with the alcohol prep pad, scrubbing vigorously a six-inch radius
for thirty seconds. I take the first needle, bend the butterfly-like
wings back, poised in my right hand.

The digital photo cube is paused on Yellow Mountain, a hike
we took five years ago. I take a deep breath. With my left hand,
I "pinch an inch" of skin as the nurses instructed, making sure
to get a good amount of subcutaneous fat, take another deep
breath, pause and hesitate. I start to insert the needle, catch
myself, try to relax, force my shoulders down.

Outdoors, the sun is shining. I am grateful for health insurance.

I breathe out, insert the needle quickly, like throwing a dart,
apply IV dressing. Only three more needles to go.

For seven hours I infuse. The pump sings its familiar song. Three
times, I stop to insert another syringe. The pump whirs and clicks.

The digital photo cube continues to cycle— Roaring Creek Falls,
Little Lost Cove Cliffs, Roan Mountain russet sedge. That night
I sleep, exhausted, my body pulling inward. I imagine the IgGs,
microbial patrols racing through my blood-stream, scouting
infectious agents, gobbling them up, fighting the war my body
cannot fight alone.

~ TWO ~

Song Sparrow

You tap on my window sill,
every morning,
align your fluffed-up feathers,
your plump little bird body
on the narrow ledge.

You hop from Dogwood
to window,
and back again.
Your gentle patter tells me
I am connected.

Sometimes

Sometimes, I do not know
how much pain
one human body can contain.

      Sparrow, wood thrush, nuthatch, phoebe,
      wren, titmouse, goldfinch, grosbeak,
      hawk, hummingbird, woodpecker, bluebird.

Sometimes, I place my hand
over my heart, feel it beating,
soothe it, hold it, bless it.

      Bluets, violets, forget-me-nots, daisies,
      lilac, roses, geranium, pansies,
      coneflower, iris, bloodroot, spirea.

Sometimes, I pause, follow my breath deeply,
crowd out all else but the movement of air,
and what is outside my window.

      Lady bug, stink bug, preying mantis, wasp,
      dragon fly, swallowtail, luna moth, ant,
      katydid, grasshopper, cricket, gnat.

Sometimes, I let the tears flow,
knowing they will soon
come again.

      Boxwood, barberry, holly, pieris,
      lilac, baby's breath, nandina, weigela,
      rose-of-Sharon, butterfly, juniper, hydrangea.

Sometimes, I imagine what would have happened if,
if not, if only, if but, and then I realize it didn't, won't,
cannot, will never.

Shag bark hickory, walnut, white oak, locust,
kousa dogwood, redbud, willow,
white pine, poplar, ironwood, sumac.

I listen, look out the window, feel, taste, breathe,
know there is enough, plenty,
indulgent feast.

Untangling Myself

I just left the doctor's office,
the only place I go these days.

Afterwards, I always drive home,
shower off the fragrance, bacteria,
put on my old clothes.

Today, I wanted to stay and visit,
take the receptionist out for lunch,
or an iced tea at the coffee shop.
Ask the nurse about her life, tell her
about mine.

I had the urge to walk into the yarn shop,
antique shop, craft shop. Saunter over
to town square. Sit on a bench, watch,
listen. Talk with someone, anyone,
everyone.

Instead, I untangled myself from the world.
Pulled myself from the excitement of town.
Shed my longing for interaction, for a moment
of activity or contact.

I started my car to head home. Crawl back
into my world of solitude and isolation.

It Hurts

It hurts to be the one
who is left home alone,
again and again.
It hurts to be the one who
cannot attend the concert,
or dinner afterwards.
It hurts to be the one who is left behind
at Easter, birthdays, Memorial Day picnics,
Mother's Day.
It is humiliating
to be the reason for cancelled plans,
for activities not attempted,
for friends who no longer visit.

It hurts to become ill
because someone visited with
a contagious virus, or lit up
a cigarette. It hurts when
people forget, fail to
understand, could modify
their choices, and don't.

It hurts that I don't know
anyone quite as isolated as I.
I look so healthy, so fine,
they fail to see my pain.

The Bucket List
with thanks to Morgan Freeman and Jack Nicholson

My list had been there
eighteen years.
A slip of card stock paper.
Embellished
with my own hand.
Doodles, hearts, flowers.
The first page
in my day planner.
A list of every place
I wanted to go.
Things I hoped to do.

I cleaned house, rampaged
closets. Gave away my suitcase,
satin pumps, rhinestone earrings.
Evening gowns I would no longer
wear, fine china I would never use.

I threw away the list.

Now, five years later, I lie in bed.
Try to reconstruct what was on
that list.

I get as far as: go to the
Grand Canyon; walk the beach
at Assateague; visit my daughters.
Remember no more.

I threw out the list. Just went on.
This strange life. Learning
not to pursue dreams.

The Body

This body is how I know myself.
Skin formed around muscle and bone
as I grew and moved, danced and swam.
This is the body that sang, made love,
gave birth, heard children laugh.

Throughout each day, five senses mark
the humbling rumble of thunder, corn silk
smoothness of silver flatware, enveloping
balm of a hot bath.

They say we are not our bodies, we are
more— the gossamer soul that lives on,
transcends.

I say it is all in the body. It is this old body
that danced with you, bends to put on shoes,
shares pizza, plays cards, holds hands.

I no longer twist tomatoes, sticky
off the vine, enjoy the confident embrace
of well-worn boots. Slippers I wear
as I shuffle from sink to desk.

When I look in the mirror it is my mother's
face I see—her wrinkles on my skin, her fat
above my elbows, her face sinking
into jowls and neck.

It is the body that is stabbed with grief,
frustration, pain, abuse, comforted by touch,
taste and sound. It is the body that celebrates,
remembers, yearns and dies.

It isn't soul I crave. It's tangible love, body love.
Hunger, for the feast of skin.

After the New Diagnosis

Everyone should be nice to me.
I want sympathy.
I want friends to call, check on me.
I want people to listen,
research my disease,
understand my suffering.

Are there any free coupons?
Do I get a day off? A free pass
to Disney World? Make-A-Wish?

Friends have never heard of my disease.
No one understands my prognosis,
my pain. There aren't pink ribbons,
not enough people for a support group.

I isolate, withdraw, avoid
saying things I need to say.
Would you please cover your mouth
when you cough? Wear a mask?
Stay home if you're sick? Restrain
your child? Your dog? Wash
your hands? Use a nail brush?
Would you please not assume
raw food, raw milk, probiotics,
are good for everyone? Could you
understand I might not always
be positive, upbeat, smiling,
interested in all your activities?

This isn't like fibromyalgia or gout.
It isn't even like cancer, which is
understood, and most likely will
go into remission.

I want a badge.
I need tenderness, empathy.
I'd really like a hug.

Your World Crashes

Your world crashes, shrinks
to the warmth of your coverlet.
Quiet descends, smothering.

You look up to the underside, come
out for air, stare blankly at the only
wall you can see.

Focus, instead, on your breath,
the sparrow outside the window,
picking at its own reflection.

You get up to use the bathroom, realize
you can barely walk, think of your to-do list,
all you would be doing today, if only.

You imagine washing windows, or even
plucking the piece of lint you saw moments
before, on the floor, when you tried to stand.

You remember your back-up list, things
to do while sick, the list you keep because
you know you will be derailed regularly.

Today, you cannot pull your energy, your mind,
to attend to any list at all. You wish a friend
would call. A friend who would hear your voice,

know how you are, sincerely ask, intently listen,
not just say you sound great. You imagine how
it might feel to speak without having to "be positive,"

"lighten up," without having to give them
"equal time." You imagine a friend coming to visit,
a friend who would know to wear a mask,

sit at a distance, talk slowly, softly listen,
limit their time, not wear you out. Not assume
you'd provide lunch. Not engage your active listening.

Not require problem-solving or advice. Someone
who would know that sitting up, smiling, listening
to trivial, unnecessary conversation is too exhausting.

Someone who would realize you simply need to be shielded
from hearing everything everyone else is doing, all their
activities, travels, worries, useless humor.

You try to imagine having a friend who would understand
you need time off, do not need to be cheered up, need
protection, reassurance, permission for rest.

You realize all you want is to exist, safely, in your own
sick place. Without having to take care of anyone else.
To be loved, for who, and how, you are.

Resentment

Some days resentment opens within me
like the main drain in the bottom of the pool,
sucking out everything that was buoyant,
leaving only the scum of negativity. I am home,

sick. My wife is at a day-long workshop, money
spent for admission, gasoline, t-shirt, book,
iced tea to-go. She is attending a friend's wedding,
needs a new dress, new shoes, wedding gift.

I cannot go. Haven't had a day off from illness,
a day away from home, in twenty-five years. I go
nowhere but the doctor's office. I reach out to others
to feel connected. Call a friend who tells me he's

attending a concert, saw an intriguing two-act play,
is planning a fishing trip. The kids call, are going
swimming, then to hunt shark's teeth on their way
to visit the other grandparents. Some days

the resentment swallows me. I lie here. Measure
the paucity of my days against the money spent,
time given to others. Always come up short.

Memorial Day Breakfast

Memorial Day weekend, I am alone.
I rise early, open the curtains to my garden
of blooming iris, daisy, rose.

Putting opera on the stereo, I dress myself
in long skirt, flowing shirt, dance through
my morning chores.

I make myself breakfast, set china on a clean
placemat with linen napkin. Poignant strains
of aria establish sanctity.

I sit down to eat next to the picture window.
The phone rings. It is Ellen calling to say
good morning. She loves me, misses me,

is listening to an audiobook while driving. Will
call me later. Phone rings. Daughter on her way
to a festival. Had a great birthday party. Misses me.

Tells me she loves me. No time to talk. Maybe
tomorrow. So much happening without me. So much
they cannot express. So much I cannot say.

I return to my breakfast. The picture window
awaits. The opera continues.
The rose still blooms.

Ode to my Eye Drops
with thanks to Sharon Olds

You sit on the top shelf of my bathroom hutch,
your pink cap unmistakable. O, Lotemax™!
O, loteprednol etabonate! It took four days for my
ophthalmologist and pharmacist to locate you, a script
lacking sulfites, polysorbate 80, sodium benzoate, a script
I could tolerate without allergic reaction, a script
that needed prior-authorization, a script that was expensive.
You are the newest item on my shelf, come to relieve
the ravages of autoimmune superior limbic keratoconjunctivitis,
which has caused pain, inflammation, blurred vision. At first
I was dismayed. Not another diagnosis! Not another condition!
But as I pondered what the loss of my vision might mean,
I postured differently, welcoming you into my life, including you
in my monthly calls to the pharmacy, my daily regimen, my closet,
my purse, my checkbook. You sit center shelf, flanked by
moisturizing and lubricating eye drops, and the rest of a closet,
that, throughout the day, I fling open to pharmaceuticals,
preparations, lotions, creams and ointments.

Your shelfmates include: nose bottle with mupirocin and budesonide,
twice daily prophylaxis for chronic sinus infections; oxymetazoline
hydrochloride for nasal hemorrhages; levalbuterol tartrate for asthma;
medications for mouth sicca and gum infections; metronidazole and
gentamicin creams for continuous complicated vaginal infections;
antibiotics for chronic urinary tract infections; creams for
neuropathy; creams for arthritis; lidocaine for ceaseless shingles pain;
powders for fungal infections; antibiotics for skin infections, incessant
infections of all varieties, in all places, to be mitigated by the little bottles
standing, lined up like little soldiers on my shelf, ready to attack
and defend what my deficient immune system cannot.

O, Lotemax™! O loteprednol etabonate! Welcome! Come live among us!
Come join the refrigerator of gamma globulin and prescribed pharmaceuticals!
Come join the closet of oxygen cylinders, injectables and infusion supplies!
Come join the kitchen cabinet of supplements and pills! Thank you
for gracing my bathroom shelf with your lovely easy-to-see pink cap!
Welcome! May our days together be long and fruitful!

Risk

Risk: A situation involving exposure to danger.
The possibility that something unpleasant
or unwelcome will happen.

My friend moved to a new house, wanted me
to see it, take a "quick run-through," opened
the windows, said there wasn't anything
in the house that would bother me. Such

a simple request. I wanted to support her.
That afternoon: sick. That night: sicker. Three
days later: still ill. This exposure to floor finish,
propane gas, glycols and urethanes, formaldehyde,

offered the probability of severe illness, for me.
My friend said she was touched I took a risk,
told others it was because I love her. Am I required
to make myself ill to show my love?

If I didn't do this, would it have meant I didn't love her?
Do I have to do this for every friend I know? Was it
easier for her to frame this as a risk, than pose another
idea? Would you ask a person in a wheelchair, to climb

a flight of stairs on their hands and knees? Would
the person climbing be ill for a week? Is it logical
to chance severe illness, for a "quick run-through?"
When I am asked, or expected, to do something that will

make me ill, I lose days, weeks, I will never have again.
When I agree to do this, a piece of self-respect
dies. I feel minimized, resentful others are going on
with their lives. I am left in a pitiful puddle of self-reproach.

Hair Loss

~ 1 ~

It started coming out in handfuls.
Three months after my hospitalization.
Telogen Effluvium was the diagnosis.
Hair was everywhere, covering my coat,
back of the car seat, shower drain,
vacuum cleaner.

First it was the long hairs. From nipple length
to collar bone in three weeks. Then, smaller pieces.
It thinned all over. Barrettes wouldn't stay in,
wouldn't even make a pony tail. Limp and lifeless,
it lost its luster, its motion. Unrecognizable
as my own, it was wispy, thin, receding, pathetic.

Hair accessories and ornaments lay obsolete
in the top drawer of my dressing table—bobby pins
and hair pins, clips of plastic, leather, ivory, wood,
brass and silver. There was no hair left to tie back,
clamp or clump. No more braids, no French twist,
no messy bun or pony tail. No options left
but a hat or scarf.

Scrapbook photos, previous years, show my hair long
or pixie cut, braided for summer camp or swimming,
sporting headbands in various sizes, thicknesses and
colors. Hair flaunting Easter bonnets, rag curlers,
up in orange juice rollers. Frizzed hippy hair, Twiggy cut,
hair with bandanas, buzz-cut dyke hair. Hair swept up
for formal occasions, pulled back in a ballet bun, hair
parted on the left, parted in the center, hair to my waist—
all unavailable with my new version of hair.

I look in the mirror while flossing my teeth.
I'm shocked at the image. Strange, not me.
I get dressed for the day. Earrings the wrong
length, hats no longer fit. From the back,
I look like a stranger. Nothing is familiar.

I prepare to meet someone new, someone
who didn't know me before I lost my hair.
I want to show them a previous photograph,
say, "See, this is the real me, this is what
I really look like." But it isn't what I look like,
now. And a photo of what I used to look like
isn't the same as sharing before-and-after photos
of eye glasses, or new makeup.

People tell me my hair looks fine. I should
accept myself as I am. But this isn't me.
The style doesn't feel like me, presents as
a different person than I am, or, than I was.
There is no hair to warm my scalp. My head
is cold. I select several yards of colorful fabric
to wrap around my head. But headscarves
aren't me, either. They're complicated.
They shift and slide off. They itch.

Hair loss, whether by chemo or sepsis, feels the same.
But hair loss from Telogen Effluvium happens without
heroism, camaraderie, or pink ribboned support.

I miss my hair. And so much else.

The Rigors of Discipline

For years, I woke each morning in the dark,
threaded my way downstairs,
set up my music stand, picked up my flute,
drilled scales, arpeggios, long tones,
rehearsed etudes, sonatas, solos,
before catching the school bus at six-fifteen.
Drill, practice, repeat.

After school, I sat on the maroon velveteen bench,
feet poised above brass pedals, fingers on the ivories,
Hannon Virtuoso Studies up and down the eighty-eight.
Drill, practice, repeat.

In the basement, a ballet barre behind the furnace,
long broom handle my father attached to the wall,
under the pegboard that held his tools. I stood at the barre,
erect, staring at the chalky cement wall, cobwebs trailing
from the ceiling, fishing poles tucked under rafters.
First position, second position, third, plié, relevé, jeté.
Drill, practice, repeat.

When illness came, bronchitis, pneumonia,
racked with fevers, I still practiced,
showed up, performed.
Drill, practice, repeat.

I push on. Every morning I shower, dress, fix my hair,
put on different earrings. Even at the hospital, I put
my feet on the floor, chin up, head pounding,
practice yoga. At home, with muscles aligned,
I carry on, thread my way to the laundry room,
the kitchen. Perform tasks. Enact the rigors of discipline.
Honor the church of the holy body, before crashing
back into bed.
Drill, practice, repeat.

Plans Derailed

~ 1~

My wife will be visiting her uncle. I will miss traveling to see family, celebrate his ninety-sixth birthday. While my wife is gone, I will have her chores to do: feed the cats, get the mail, open and shut the gate, do the dishes. It will be exhausting, but I will maintain my health regimen, schedule and isolation, which isn't the same as maintaining my health.

While my wife is gone, I hope to suckle my sick self with other pleasures, look forward to the food she cooked, stacked in labeled containers in the fridge. I will savor the silence, enjoy a hot bath, good book, edit some poetry, stretch out over the entire bed. I will relish some out-of-routine days, luxuriate in my own Class-B "vacation."

~ 2 ~

The trip didn't happen. After I helped with her suitcase, cut her hair, made a birthday card and wrapped his gifts, I crumbled. Got sick, had to get in bed, talk to doctors. My prepared meals were now brought on a tray. My wife cancelled her plans, unpacked, got refunds. I sipped electrolytes, warm tea. I took naps, needed more blankets, extra pillows.

She checked on me, sat with me. On the third day, I felt well enough to realize what had happened. The trip had been cancelled and I was the reason. I had caused disappointment and inconvenience. I felt like a failure, felt shame with my body, it's frailty. Felt guilty, thankful for her ministrations.

On the fourth day, I realized it wasn't just my wife and family that lost out. I had lost out, too; my own plans had been obliterated. I had lost the trip, and my second-class sick plans. There had been no hot bath, no writing, no reading stretched out on the bed. My solitude had been consumed, again, by medical crisis. But my losses seemed invisible.

My sadness paled in comparison to theirs, could not be understood. I sat in a slump, drifting off. Silently, I grieved my derailed plans. I didn't want to be the one nursed and pitied. I would have been content to spend my days unassisted, delighting in my solitude, appreciatively succoring myself with what is left. Alone.

~ THREE ~

This is a Poem about Illness

This is a poem about illness, chronic illness, the almost daily,
        regular transitioning between standing upright,
        and quickly having to lie down.

This is a poem about the sudden shift of energy, the minute
        it happens, the moment illness descends like an axe,
        nausea that rolls in like a sea surge, stomach cramps,
        mind-splitting headaches, the dullness of mind that engulfs
        my faculties, blood pressure that drops, causing me to stop
        whatever I am doing, forcing me to lie down, wherever
        I may be.

This is a poem about the moment illness reasserts itself, spreads
        like poison, moves stealthily in my veins, my body again
        under siege.

This is a poem about feeling sick, being sick, febrile, fatigued,
        infected, foreign mitochondria multiplying in my lymph glands,
        attack of the body trappers, systemic illness that subverts
        my days, will not relent, will not remit.

This poem about illness, about the kind of illness that is invisible.
        The kind where you aren't in a wheelchair, the kind you don't
        post on Facebook, the kind that isn't self-inflicted, isn't karma,
        isn't cancer, won't respond to organic food, acupuncture or
        B-vitamins, will not heal from healthy air, positive thinking,
        quiet music, or meditation.

This poem about illness is beyond all the excellent doctors I see,
        the arrogant doctors I have endured, beyond my seven-hour
        infusions of immune globulin, beyond the pills I take, the
        expensive modifications I must make.

This is a poem about being disabled by chronic sickness, being disabled
        because I am too ill to work, too ill for accommodation, too
        chronic for a get-well card, a life that never got off the ground,
        a life arrested, truncated.

This poem is about learning to forgive my own body, about every choice
        I make that is held up to my own scrutiny: can I really do what
        I would like, without harm? Is what I want to do really worth
        the price I will pay?

This poem is about every profession for which I trained and studied,
        every talent which I developed and can no longer employ.

This poem is about every bucket list I ever had, every desire, plan
        and responsibility I had to relinquish.

This is a poem about not expecting to be understood, except
        by my spouse, my daughter, one friend, and only
        some physicians.

This illness is the reason there aren't more poems written, more visits
        enjoyed, more books read, the reason there aren't concerts,
        vacations, volunteer activities, or bank accounts.

This is a poem about loss, about so much that hasn't happened
        and won't, about lost opportunities, trade-offs, trade-downs,
        setbacks, knockdowns.

This is a poem about learning to let go of so much, really letting go,
        saying goodbye to what I had, what I held, what I did,
        what I wanted, to watch it all move away, recede, evaporate.

This is a poem about knowing the family gathers without me,
        about the weddings, graduations, and recitals I will not attend,
        knowing there are grandchildren I have not met, daughters
        I rarely see, realizing the dreams I had for retirement
        and old age, will not happen.

This poem is about learning to open my heart and hear, repeatedly,
every place they go, where I cannot, every class, meeting,
party, and workshop they will attend, and I will not.

This poem is about listening to details of every vacation he takes,
every restaurant she visits, every store she shops, knowing
I am home, with four subcutaneous needles in my abdomen,
the third day this week.

This is a poem about choosing not to feel marginalized when I am
a resource for others who are not a resource for me. When
I listen to activities others can do, which I cannot.

This poem is about the courage it takes to say, "No, I cannot
meet you for lunch," and, "No, I cannot travel to your home,"
and not succumb to guilt or despair, while trying to frame it
in positive language, and keep a smile on my face.

This poem is about trying to remain forgiving and up-beat while
knowing I will spend energy I do not have, take risks I cannot
afford, to entertain friends who will not understand my
boundaries.

This poem about illness, is a poem about learning to be grateful for
small things, the rare day, the rare conversation, small
kindnesses that include, approach and soothe.

This illness poem is about listening to all the things people say,
the judgments and misunderstandings, recommendations
for another practitioner, suggestions for supplements, made
by those who do not even know the name of my illness,
or understand its extent.

This is a poem about bucking up when people tell me I look too good
to be *seriously ill*, or that my illness is too *negative*, too *painful*
to hear, that I certainly must be *depressed*.

This is a poem about overlooking when others cannot comprehend
how I can enjoy a rich and full spiritual life, or think they are
more enlightened, "have it all together," or are "doing it right,"
because they are not suffering from a genetic illness.

This is a poem about using discrimination in selecting friends,
discernment in what I choose to disclose, deciding what
I cannot say to those who will not listen.

This poem is about moving forward, all the "try again," "get-up-again,"
"start-over-again," all the explanations one-more-time,
to one-more-person.

This poem is as much about frustration, grief, longing, jealousy,
and resentment, as it is about courage, love, willpower,
self-control and determination.

This is a poem about surviving an illness that cuts to the bone,
to the gut, the brain, the immune system, the nerve endings.

This is a poem about an illness I endure, knowing
I am fully alive, singing, "Hallelujah,"
through my ever-present tears.

Nights

It is on nights, such as this,
when I cannot get comfortable
in a chair, in bed, and no soft
words, touch, or extra pillows,
will help –

It is on nights, such as this,
when the raw dagger of pain
races up my spine, down my legs,
across my pelvis, every muscle
and sinew braced—

It is on nights, such as this,
when all my friends are at a party,
that I wonder why I don't take
the car and drive to Las Vegas,
fuck nameless others, die
in some accident, walk in
the mountains, freeze
in the cold, or take a room
at a hotel, down an entire bottle
of pills and simply fade away.

It is on nights such as this
I remember despair doesn't
arrive with the dawn,
but occurs at night.

Another Day

I can barely move.
It is evening. The thrush sings.

Dampness rolls in
through my window.

It seems, only a few minutes
ago, the same song,

of the same bird, woke me
to another day.

Time moves on, suspended
between bed clothes. My skin

is hot, lips parched, head thick,
eyes burning in my sockets. I am

thankful for a cool drink,
clean sheets, a kind smile.

To my Friend at the Beach

On my calendar I have a note that you begin your second
round of chemo, tomorrow. You called last week, from
Dewey Beach, left a message on my answering machine.
I was too ill to talk, slugging out another infection.

Early this morning, the cats shrieked. Their urgent plight
brought me to their immediate assistance. An unknown
intruder had turned over their water bowl, sending them
to the trees for safety. The cats are fine, now. They have

gone on with their day, sit quietly, content on a rock
in the sun. You are fine, too, after your first month of chemo.
Even with cancer, you seem to be thriving, now that they have
arrested the lymphoma. Also on my calendar this week,

is the anniversary of my last vacation, the vacation that proved
I am too ill to travel. After thirty years of debilitating symptoms,
I am no longer a medical emergency. My illness
is part of the landscape, mostly

overlooked. Cancer is not the only serious illness. I am sorry
you have cancer, but you aren't even ill. You are not the only
friend who has struggled with cancer. Most continue to live.
Only a few have died. What you all share is the heroic,

socially-supported experience of cancer. I have nurtured
and listened to all of you, while you have vacationed
and pursued your bucket lists. For me, there are no pink
ribbons, no support groups, phone trees, get well cards,

volunteers coming to hold my hand, or bring dinner. Why
are your PET scans and chemo treatments on my calendar?
Why are my infusions not on yours? Why are your treatments
given the gift of calls and cards, and you do not even know

I have debilitating infusions three times a week? I know where
you are, how you are, and what you are doing. You have no idea
how I am, or even the name of my illness. Each of us moves
towards death in different ways, some recognized, supported,

urgent and noticed. Others of us die slowly, loss by loss,
surrendering to the silence, unsupported, isolated, invisible.
I haven't returned the message you left last week from
Dewey Beach. You will return, go out to dinner, have friends

visit, continue your beneficial treatments, while planning
your next trip. The cats are still preening in the sun. Sick in bed,
I haven't been able to stretch across the chasm.

Hope

I do not know if I will ever see
the Grand Canyon, stone lighthouse
at Ocracoke, Colorado Mountains,
or my children grow to maturity.

I do not know if I will ever travel
to Provincetown for a vacation,
our dream house in the country,
my daughter's graduation.

And yet, each morning
I roll over to greet
your deep eyes,
warm flesh,

hopeful the day may bring
a new bird to our feeder,
or the unfolding
of some new blossom.

The Veil of Silence

Richard left yesterday for Hilton Head. Sarah
is excited about their cruise. David is in Annapolis.
My girls are at the Outer Banks with their father.
Leslie just visited her kids. Douglas leaves tomorrow.

I listen to their plans. Their dreams.
Long to share mine.

Today, Douglas said he could not do what I do,
doesn't know how I cope. I didn't tell him. Didn't
offer the details. Gave the short version. Told him
I meditate, sing, pay attention to what is outside
my window, which bird is on which tree, phase
of the moon, direction of the wind.

I told him I do this to feel connected. Keep it
simple. Keep it light. Remember there are other
realities. My life is not the center.

I am not brave. Do what I have to do.
Survive behind the veil of silence.

Lunch at the Clinic

Sitting in the lobby between appointments, I have isolated
myself in a corner to avoid others, establish a buffer of
safety. Trying to eat my lunch, sanitized hands, vinyl gloves,

face mask removed momentarily. In walks a family,
grandmother, mother, small toddler. The curious child
comes over. My safety shield, personal boundaries, are

broached. We pick up our lunch, our bags, move to another
corner. The curious child follows, wants to engage.
The parents think he is cute. We do not. We are worried

about viral exposure from little children carrying contagious
illness. We politely smile at the parents, explain I am
immune deficient, must not be around small children.

How odd it might seem that we must retreat, are not
amused by a small child. Please don't take it personally,
we say, as we pack our bags, gracefully exit.

How Are You Doing?

"Hello, Mrs. McVicker.
How ya doin' today?"

"Just fine. I'm just fine.
Just hanging in there."

I'm lying here on the floor
with my back brace on.
My life always seems
to be falling apart
as I struggle to hold together
body, mind, soul,
bank account,
aging automobiles,
and relationships.

But, I'm fine.
Really, I'm fine.

I used to think
that when someone
posed this question
they wanted the truth.

Later,
I thought no one
ever wanted
the truth.

Now,
my perspective is
people ask this question
because they are
similarly
mired in life.

They are desperately
clinging to the same thread
I clench in my teeth.

This question, when posed,
is not rhetorical, perfunctory,
or insincere.

"How are you," antecedent,
and, "I'm fine," consequent,
the great equalizers,
what all our lives
boil down to,
the syrup that remains
at the bottom of the pot,
the moment of awareness:
I am alive,
I am fine.

Celebrate the Body

Celebrate the body that stands when you bid.
Holds there, moves left, right, back. Without reeling
off into vertigo. Without tremors, shakes, pauses, falls.

Celebrate the body that breathes without wheezes.
Without pneumonia, rales, rhonchi. The heart that pumps.
Blood pressure that adjusts, fluctuates to provide assistance
without faltering, racing, palpitating.

Celebrate the mouth that receives food. Lips and tongue
that coordinate swallowing. Esophagus that receives, delivers
to the stomach which digests freely. Peristalsis moving
contents without steatorrhea, diarrhea, distension, malabsorption.

Celebrate the brain which processes, remembers, understands.
Thinks, reasons, considers, knows, ponders, grasps. Postulates
without scramble, confusion, lapses or gaps.

Celebrate the senses, which pleasure at the soothe of touch,
the rouse of music, connection of language, clarity of vision,
grounding of taste, cathedral of aroma. Senses that do not bring
the slap of pain which overwhelms, frightens, disengages, disconnects,
humiliates, blurs. Which cuts off, isolates, confuses, erases meaning.

Consider love. Consider relationship, beauty, meaning, purpose.
Celebrate the music heard from the other room. The owl hooting
at night. Coyotes calling from the hill. The pleasant nurse who makes
eye contact, offers a laugh, a smile. Imagine the tenderness of hair
stroked off the back of a neck. Something personal said because you
were a person before being a patient. You were a person with dreams
and wants, desires and fantasies. Not just the depositor of medical
waste in sharps containers. Before you watched friends withdraw.

Then consider the body in illness. Lengthy illness that does not retract.
Does not go into remission. The body locked in a vice-grip. Unable

to be healed, understood, or even accepted. Consider how everything is reduced to needle sticks, lab cultures, pills, ointments, liniments. Layers of blankets, modifications, isolation. A person on bed rest, house arrest. Scrutinized, controlled by insurance and medical tyranny.

Consider the raw, raked emotion of this sick person. Ratcheted with exhaustion. On the edge of an abyss. Future uncertain. Agitation, irritation, humiliation. Grievous anger, jealousy, disgust. Feeling lost, afraid, anxious, needy. Trying to contain, control, subdue. Trying to be normal, act normal, perceived as normal, treated as normal, remembered as normal. Once again to just to be normal.

Consider how little things become important. The cup that has a straw or doesn't. The blanket that is straight or haphazard. The windows that are too open or too shut. Blinds that allow too much glare or not enough light. The upside-down tray. The forgotten gesture, harsh word, sudden loud noise. The lengthy conversation, too many demands, or not enough.

Consider this body. So much, for so long. Not enough, for too long. So much beauty, so much pain and loss. Joys and hopes filled and dashed. Life and death, handled simultaneously.

Speak of It

We, who are chronically ill, do not
speak of it, do not speak of death.

There are millions lost before, the vast company
of the dead. This knowledge reduces my terror

of nothingness. I know it is normal to feel what I feel.
But we do not speak of it. Instead, discussion

revolves around the lives of others, their activities.
Or, we briefly mention my infections, medical

appointments. But we do not speak of death, do not speak
of fear. I remain intact, composed, knowing how it will all

end, while wanting to scream. Everyone knows how it will
end, thinking but never admitting they are glad it is me,

and not them. I am intent upon surviving as long as I can,
with pain, energy disappearing, body parts dissolving.

I remain focused, stay calm in the moments that do not
seem to end. But will.

Please, Let them Find a Tumor

Please, let them find a tumor,
let it be an infected organ, a kink
of bowel. Oh! There it is!

No wonder you've been so ill!
All we need is to start an IV drip!
Perform surgery! Excise this lump!

Please, let them find something tangible.
Something they can fix, something that,
once removed, will restore me to health,
or something that will take me soon,
something that gives me just enough time
to plan my funeral, say goodbye, know
the suffering will be over.

Please, don't let it be more of the same,
more infection, immune deficiency,
autoimmune, pain.

Please, let it be something easy, something
they can fix, or something that takes me quick.
Something that ends.

Isn't fifty years
of chronic illness
enough?

Things People Say

You sure don't look sick!

> *Yes! It took me three hours of preparing my hair and make-up*
> *to pull this off! Just because I don't look sick, doesn't mean*
> *I am not. I'm glad my outsides don't match my insides!*
> *If I looked the way I feel, I'd scare small children!*

I'm sorry. I'm SO sorry. You poor thing!

> *Sorry for what? Did you do something? You're sorry? That my life*
> *sucks? That I'm the one down? That you certainly don't envy me?*

You're so brave! You're such an inspiration! I can't imagine living like you do!

> *I'm so glad my life is an inspiration for others! Do I have to act normal*
> *and be an inspiration, too? Do I have to stay on my pedestal? Can I still*
> *have my crabby days?*

Your wife must be a saint! You're so lucky to have her! Too bad for her!

> *Yes, I guess she just has to put up with me! Poor thing.*
> *And I don't ever do a thing for her!*

Well, God doesn't give you anything you can't handle.

> *I'm so glad you told me that!*

I know how you feel, I had the flu last week. Are you sick enough to
actually be in bed?

> *If I stayed in bed because I'm sick, I'd always be in bed! My chronic*
> *illness won't go away. This isn't the flu, and I won't be better in a week.*
> *I can't just take a few days off. I have to push and crash, push and crash.*

I have a friend who had what you have, but he got better!

> *Well, lucky him! Despite the best medical care in the world,*
> *that didn't happen to me! I guess I don't have what your friend had!*

What is your weight today?

> *You have no business asking me that question! I didn't realize my weight*
> *was a matter of public discourse! Can we discuss your weight, too?*

I'm feeling pretty good today! I hope you are, too!

> *I'm glad you're feeling good today! It's a pretty good bet that I am not!*

My cheerful demeanor does not mean I'm feeling great!

You do more in a day than I can manage! Perhaps you're not as sick as you say.
> *If you don't get more done, maybe you are just lazy! You, deciding*
> *what my activity level should or should not be, with an illness, is unfair.*
> *Yes, I do a lot of seemingly impossible tasks, in spite of my illness.*
> *Otherwise, my tasks would not get done. I'm not going to feel better, so*
> *I've figured out how to accomplish things, even while ill. I'm not tied*
> *to the bed. I know I have incredible determination, discipline and will*
> *power. Aren't I amazing?*

What doesn't kill you only makes you stronger!
> *Then I must be pretty damn strong! I'm sure if you were faced with this,*
> *you'd find out you have more strength than you think!*

It must be great to take a nap in the middle of the day. I sure
wish I could! You're so lucky you don't have to work!
> *I'd love to go back to work! That would mean I'd be healthy enough*
> *to do other fun things, like go visit friends or go out to dinner!*
> *I loved my job and having a decent income! Staying home is*
> *no vacation! I hate being sick and having to take naps!*

I don't want to hear this! This is depressing! It's negative! Just be positive!
I'll pray for you!
> *I'll take the prayers! "Being positive" hasn't worked yet; I'm having to go*
> *with "being realistic." I'd be happy for you to call me once in a while,*
> *just listen to me, or come help out! I'm not asking you to be my*
> *therapist.*

Well, things COULD be worse. Just be glad you don't have CANCER!
> *Yes, it could be worse! I am so glad I don't have cancer!*
> *But I am not convinced that cancer IS worse. I know a lot of friends*
> *living with cancer, who have more health, freedom, and energy*
> *than I could muster.*

Feel better soon!
> *OK! I'm looking forward to that! But I don't think that is going to happen.*
> *And I'm not being negative! I have a chronic illness that isn't going away,*
> *and won't go into remission. I'm in this for life.*

You Old Dog

You old dog,
you fell four times today,
walked into the fence,
stumbled over nothing.

You whine more these days,
sleep more,
snuggle more.

You, old dog,
are my closet friend.
We come in, we go out.
We breathe and eat in tandem.

You come to me, head bowed,
and lean in, close.
I read your thoughts.
You listen to mine.

Who knows
how much longer
we have.

We will be parted only
when one of us
dies.

Then, the other
will be left,
to cry her tears
alone.

To my Friend with Cancer

You don't have it anymore! You tell me
you have "no evidence of active disease."

You will return every three months for a CT
or PET scan, sometimes an MRI. You always

let Facebook know your anxiety before the scans.
You send group texts afterwards, telling us

"It was clear!" We breathe a sigh of relief, send
"Thumbs Up!" You go on another vacation, sit

by the ocean, drink cocktails, enjoy company,
eat at restaurants, pursue your Bucket List.

Imagine if your doctor had said, "There's
not much we can do." Imagine if your doctor

had said, "What you have is very rare. There
really isn't anything anyone can do, but we

will refer you to someone who will manage
your condition." You would know the doctor

meant exactly what he said. There wouldn't be
anything they could do. Someone would "manage"

you until you would die. How would you feel?
What would you say on Facebook? Would you

feel you could say anything on Facebook, if you
didn't have cancer? You told me you felt "ripped off"

about the eight months you lost to surgery and
chemotherapy. Eight months. Can you even imagine

what it might feel like to be "ripped off" by the last
fifty years of chronic illness? You are in remission.

I am not.

Returning Home after Three Weeks at the Clinic
A List Poem

Dark laundry, white laundry, silks, hand wash.
Rewash, hang out, take down, sort.
Fold, put away sleeping bags, duffle bags.
Clean the car, the trunk. Reorganize purse, backpack.
Reorder, replenish, replace.
Infuse.

~

Retrieve mail from the post office. Read, sort,
throw away, file. Answer mail, pay bills, return calls, file.
Realize Blossman overcharged us. Call Blossman.
Realize Accredo hasn't been paid by Cigna. Call Cigna.
Realize Medicare appeal was denied again. Call Medicare.
Infuse.

~

Boot up computer, get online. Ethernet isn't working.
Shut down, reboot, try again, later.
Download email, sort email, trash email, answer email.
Balance check book, catch up register, pay bills online.
Infuse.

~

List expenditures, organize receipts, add up, file.
Replenish emergency cash. Order pharmaceutical refills.
Order vitamins and supplements.
Infuse.

~

Catch up medical records. Get on patient portal. Download
medical records, print. Discover printer isn't working.
Fix printer. Print, copy, collate, file. Compile cover letter
for local physicians. Include office notes, stuff envelopes,
stamp and mail.
Infuse.

~

Catch up on personal phone calls. Figure out
new medication schedule. Write in journal.
Make another to-do list.
Infuse.

~

I Called to Ask You a Question

I promised I'd get this document to you, and I will.
I know there's a deadline. I agreed to do it. I've called
to ask you a question. I see I have awakened you
from your afternoon nap. Now, you're telling me

it doesn't have to be done today. Of course it does.
I have to print up the damn document and get it
in the mail. The computer died this morning.
I've been uninstalling, reinstalling programs

to abort a physical-memory-dump, a conflict
in updated drivers for software that is too old.
I am working frantically. Beets are boiling over on the
stove, the dryer is chiming, clothes are ready to fold.

The bed sits naked, ready for clean sheets. The dog
shit on the floor. I haven't had lunch and it's four o-clock.
I cannot stand one more voice on the phone, awakened
from a nap, home from a vacation, going out to dinner,

on a cruise, watching a movie, telling me to kick-back,
slow down, ease up, let go. I cannot kick-back.
Leisure time has been allocated as unfairly as health,
financial resources, and family support.

If I let things go I'll never get caught up. It's easy
for you to project your leisure onto my life, easy for you
to tell me what to do. I am managing chronic illness,
low income, fifty acres, and an incontinent dog.

I feel like an overworked hamster, solitary in my cage,
madly spinning, running between frantic survival needs
and care of my health. What is it you do not understand?
When the dishes pile up, dog slips in poop on the floor,

there's no food prepared, the laundry is in the dryer,
bed unmade, when I'm on the floor, sores weeping
with infection, I know you won't be the one to come
help me get back on track.

Alone at Night

Shouldered with a blanket
Shuttered by the window
Rain pouring   Misty moist drenching
Scent of wet leaves   Earthworms
Thinking of my death   By infection
By shingles   By loneliness   By hunger for touch
With meaningless   Empty hope
Writing words   On endless pieces of paper
As pens retire   To the trash

I cry tears   Try to move on   Go forward
Smile   Make meaning
Make sense   Of anything

~ FOUR ~

In the Photograph

In the photograph, the granddaughter holds a bouquet
at her piano recital. Her family surrounds, arms around,
well-dressed, smiling, congenial. In the picture you see
her mother, father, younger brother, infant cousin,

grandfather, aunts, uncles, cohesively gathered, embracing
this important moment. You do not see the chronically ill
grandmother. This grandmother, who was a professional
musician, is missing. This grandmother, in the weeks before,

talked with her granddaughter, listened to her worries, offered
tips on handling nervousness, making eye-contact with the
audience, what to do during applause, or if she made a mistake.
This grandmother wanted to attend, but could not. She performed

invisible work, lit a candle prior to the recital. This grandmother
was not present at the gathering, was not included in the family
snapshot, in her granddaughter's scrapbook. This grandmother
will not be visible. It is as if she is lost. Lost to history.

Even in the timelessness of the photograph.

Nursing my Solitude

I received a text. The wedding was over.
The organist played Widor's Toccata and Fugue
as a postlude.

I walked outside, put the cats' bowl away.
They came out from under the shed to see if
I'd give them another treat. I sat down
on the swing in my old sweatshirt and tattered shorts.

With all the upheaval for months-- dresses, shoes,
invitations, menus, travel plans-- you would
have thought there would be something
outside to announce the fact.

Around me nothing momentous had happened.
All was quiet, everything was the same, nothing
had changed. The world was silent, intact.
A gentle breeze blew up the hollow.

My wife and children were elsewhere. I was not.
I sat there, nursing my solitude, same as I had
for so many other weddings, births, funerals.
Same as I had for each day, for many years.

The evening chill set in. I returned to the house.
Sat down at the piano. Played Bach's sixth invention,
followed by Beethoven's Opus 27. Finished quietly
with Rachmaninoff.

Silence

It is quiet. A cricket chirps
outside in the tall grass
of the pasture. A bee buzzes
at the window screen. The dog
shifts her position on the floor,
as the refrigerator compressor
clicks on, clicks off. Once
in a while the ice maker
empties itself of frozen chunks
and refills.

Other than that, it is quiet.

I do my chores, care for myself,
fold laundry, empty the dishwasher,
conduct business, walk the dog,
nurse various projects, read,
sew, write.

Some days I am sicker than others.
Many days I am too sick to do much.
Still, it is quiet. Sometimes the phone
rings. If I am able, I answer it.
Afterwards, the silence resumes.

Today, the quietness is tinged
with nostalgia, the memory
of when I was never lonely,
a memory that knows
the silence will continue

Riding in the Car

I rode twelve hours yesterday
Front passenger seat back
As far as it would go   Feet up
On the dashboard   Leaning back

Afghan, maps, over my lap   Pillow
Under my head   Co-piloting   Pen rolls
Under the seat   I reach for it   Maps fall
Can't reach them   Pillow falls

Have to reassemble   Everything   Still no pen
The air is stale   Skin aches   Throbs
I am thirsty   Hungry   Want to cry   Sleep
Nuzzle   Run   Push   Beyond some physicality

I can no longer   Muster   I collapse   Into retreat
Suck it all in   Disconnect   Quell the fire   Sit in this
Painful body   Move through   This bleak terrain
With so many miles   So many days   Ahead

Double Crochet

In the midst of my feverish life,
I lie on the window seat.

> *J. & P. Coats "Big Ball" Best Six Cord,*
> *Mercerized Crochet Cotton, Size 30.*

Ice packed along my painful spine,
we are waiting for company to arrive.

> *Crochet Hook, No. 10.*
> *Attach thread securely to cut piece. Chain 3.*

I am unable to participate in preparations,
unable to work my chores.

> *Single crochet in 2nd chain from hook,*
> *chain 3, skip 2 chain,*
> *in next chain make (single crochet, chain 6) twice,*
> *and single crochet. Repeat.*

Supportive pillows tucked in around me,
each vertebra immobile on ice,
all I can do is return phone calls, read,
problem-solve, or crochet small items.

> *Single crochet in first single crochet*
> *and in first chain-3 loop.*
> *(Chain 3, single crochet in next chain-6 loop) twice;*
> *chain 3, (single crochet in next chain-3 loop) twice;*
> *Repeat.*

I have a size 10 steel hook in my hand
repairing the doily
my grandmother made for me
forty years ago.

> *Do not turn. Working along opposite side,*
> *single crochet in first chain, repeat first row.*
> *Chain 1, turn.*
> *Repeat 2nd row.*

I repair the frayed pattern,
replicate her stitches,
refashion this heirloom.

> *Chain 9. Turn.*
> *Skip first chain–3 space,*
> *in next chain–3 space make double crochet,*
> *chain 3 and double crochet.*

My grandmother sat on her couch with me,
taught me to hold the hook,
see the patterns,
decipher this language
of handwork.

> *Chain 3, skip next 2 chain–3 spaces.*
> *In next chain–3 space*
> *make double crochet,*
> *Chain 3 and double crochet.*
> *Repeat.*

How comforting to retreat
into these places
of love.

> *End with chain 3,*
> *treble–treble in last single crochet.*
> *Break off and fasten.*

Ellen's Lament to the Children

Don't you understand   I cannot come visit
The willow is green   The dogwood casts
A white sheen   In the moonlight
Ferns unfurl   Their tender heads

Don't you understand   I cannot come and stay
The grass is high   In the meadow
Road bars   Are full of silt
Potatoes   Are not planted

Don't you understand   The moon is full
Life is short   Your mama   Is always ill
And I   Have only now   Come to claim
The place we live   As home

Don't you understand   I cannot be away too long
Have spent so many years   Away   Far too much
Never home   Never here   Never doing   What needed doing
What I wanted   What I miss   What I long for

Don't you understand   Cities hold   No mystery   For me
Except groceries   I am older   Sicker   More tired
The smell   The noise   The traffic   Lights   Sounds   Busyness
Wear me down   Make me sick   Remove the ground   From under me

Don't you understand   I love you more   Than ever before
But I cannot come   Be there   Even for the grandchildren
Must be home   Who knows   How much time there is
The potatoes   Need to be planted   The goats   Are bleating in the barn

Don't you understand   Life narrows   At sixty-three
There is just less and less   I want to do   And more   I just want to be
Here   And tend   Nurture   There is so little time
And your mother   Oh your mother   And I   Are doing just fine

Don't you understand   Visiting you   Is painful   For the possibilities
That didn't happen   The past   That slipped by   The people   No longer there

The children   Grown up   The old   Departed   The homes sold   Jobs ended
Time   That seeped through my fingers   Before the tomatoes even bloomed

Don't you understand   That was all then   And the now   That is happening
Will not come again   And I must be   Where I am   Before it is too late
For what is calling me   To plant   Dig   Weed   Hoe   Kiss   Talk   Listen
For what is calling me   To hike   Smell   Watch   Wait   Touch   Love

As for Life

with thanks to Mary Oliver

As for life,
I am grateful for the winter comforter
cocooning me near the autumn window.

As for life,
I am left with memory and words
clotted with grief, knotted in my throat,
even desire's wings, clipped.

As for life,
it has been difficult, the rending of work
and home, not able to float in a still pool,
alone, or receive comfort from the dear dog
whose brown eyes looked into mine, or sit
with others across the table and share
a bottle of wine.

As for life,
every day I put on earrings, as if something
is happening. I am not ready for death.
Mary Oliver asks if I can't wait to be
a hummingbird. I do not want to be a
hummingbird. I have only wanted my one life,
this one chance.

Illness is a River

with thanks to Barbara Crooker

Illness   Is a river   Into which many wade
Finally get   To the other side
I am in the middle   Wet socks pulling me
Not enough strength   To move upstream
Or down   Stuck here   Mossy rocks
Mist floating   Autumn leaves   Cascading
I know I cannot get   To the other side
Must learn   To be content   Here
Watching others   Arrive safely
Huddle around   The bonfire
Family   Friends
I must linger here   Ignore
The icy numbness   Creeping   Up my legs

They may talk with me   On their way past
They do not tarry   Do not understand
How it feels   To be here   Alone
Growing cold   Weak
It is all mine   I cannot cross over
Until   It's all   Over

Complicated Grief Never Ends

Grief arrives every day, saying, "I am here; I will not leave; you will deal with me every day, all the days you have left," and then is silenced, momentarily, by a sunset, a symphony, a smile, a caress, a voice on the phone, a slip of citrus biting the tongue.

Accepting grief in one hand, hope in the other, hope which doesn't mean holding out for a miracle, hope which doesn't mean living on the bright-sided, unfounded drug of optimism,

but hope that embraces the black-eyed Susans smiling from the vase, the steaming eggs over easy, breeze coming up the cove through the window, cats purring on the porch, the full moon waking me at night, shining on the bed.

Complicated grief never ends. There is grief we cannot get over, unattenuated grief, ambiguous grief, the sweet and utter emptiness of missing loved ones, dead, absent to dementia, unable to visit, missing in action.

Health scenarios that cannot be healed. Situations with no solution. Divorce, poverty, immigration, chronic illness, the Holocaust, Civil War, genocide, terrorism. There is no closure to joy, to hope, or to love. There is no closure to grief, or loss.

To hold suffering is to acknowledge loss to ourselves, to each other. To hold suffering is to seize life by the shoulders and say "I see you." To simply say, "We have so much in common; more than we ever knew."

After I'm Gone

Before I'm lost to time and illness
I want to say I had a full life, slept
out in the rain, paddled canoes,
swam laps, danced all night.

Before I'm lost to time and illness,
I want to say I hiked miles of trails,
worked on my car, played my flute,
wrote poetry, sang songs.

Before I'm gone, I want you to know
I loved crowds and concerts, Courvoisier
and chocolate, loved clean sheets,
a good laugh, new earrings.

Before I'm lost to time and illness,
I want to say there was never enough,
so much left undone, so much more
I wanted to do.

After I'm gone, I hope you remember
I knew how to embroider intricate patterns,
design and build houses, listen to friends,
solve problems, express myself with words.

After I'm gone, I will haunt you every time
you pick up a salamander, find a spider,
sleep in a tent, pee in the woods, paddle
down the river.

After I'm gone, I hope you enjoy campfires,
the Sunday bacon, authentic communication,
music, poetry, appreciate your good health,
love each other.

After I'm gone, I hope you know I will be there
every time you listen to Moonlight Sonata, hike
a trail, dive into a pool, hear katydids, consider
your own face in the mirror.

When I am Dead
with thanks to Christina Rossetti

When I am dead   My dearest
I hope you sell the farm
Buy that Airstream you've wanted
And without a goddamn or a darn
Drive into the dream
Drive to a blue state
Seize your own fate
Ask someone beautiful
On a date

I will not see the shadows
I will not feel the rain
But you can have a life
Can live beyond the pain

And riding through the sunset
Continuing on your path
Happily you will remember
Or happily   You'll forget

The Wood Thrush

Rising from the dusk, clear
as a nightingale. Behold!

An unaccompanied song emerges
from under the forest cathedral.

Melodious soprano executes complex trills,
towers over all other sounds.

I am called from my bed, barefoot,
to the deck. It is the thrush!

I have lived through the winter.
Enjoined this moment.

I shudder at the magnificence.
Surrender in astonishment.

My enraptured heart
opens.

What Comes Next

I remember getting out of the shower
at age eleven, tossing my hair, donning
underwear, t-shirt, pair of shorts, throwing
my towel over the rod, and running downstairs.

At age fifteen, more painstaking work
on the hair at the mirror, before
running downstairs.

At age twenty-one, I remember the confidence,
working smoothly like dance steps, start to finish,
emerging fresh.

At thirty-five, the procedure shorter, sure
of myself, no longer needing to focus
on make-up or hair, it fell into place
with wonder and grace.

At forty-five I arranged a chair, the fallback
for faintness after a bath, drying off one leg
at a time, holding on to the ladder-back.

At fifty, I needed the chair, not to hold on,
not to assist, but to sit,
while beads of sweat dripped.

At fifty-five I dismissed the towel, hastily
threw on a robe, plopped down on the bed,
opened a book, and read.

Today, at sixty-five, I did the same, lay
on the bed, pulse banged in my head,
ready to pull a book off the shelf, when
a voice inside said:

Oh, can't I just lay here? Do I have to read?
Can't I just breathe the after-bath cleanness?
Can't I just shut my eyes and doze off for a while?
Whatever is next, could it possibly wait?

I imagine death like this, the logical succession,
what comes next, the flesh heavier, the exquisite
flight of just laying down the body, the agenda,
the quieting of desire for anything else
but the present.

I shut my eyes, this instant of bliss, enraptured
by the sweet moment of this clean body on the bed,
sun coming through eyelids so calm, wetness of hair,
smell of soap.

Volley of Darkness

The chill breath of evening,
spiced with wood smoke,
curls in the window.
I turn on the amber lamp,
soothe dark corners.
Open the cast iron door,
strike a match,
light the wood stove.
A barred owl
hoots a low tone,
answered by another,
on the other side of our cove.
A volley of eerie whispers.
I sit down, arrange a pillow
on my highback rocker.
Wrap the tattered afghan
tightly around my legs.
Tend the yearning
that opens as a chasm
when darkness falls.

I Leave Behind
with thanks to Wendell Berry

I leave behind my walking stick.
I leave behind working in the garden,
hiking in the woods.
I leave behind swimming.
I leave behind taking classes
in a room full of others.
I leave behind shopping, restaurants,
concerts, plays, workshops.
I leave behind dreams of performing,
ever, again.
I leave behind so much I wanted,
so much I want, still.

But the wren still sings on the porch rail,
hummingbirds still come to the feeder.
The turkeys cluck on the hill,
preying mantis cling to the window screen.
The spider spins a web in the corner.
There is much to notice. My body,
the earth itself, even the comforter
as it contains my grief. All of them
without cost, complimentary, a gift.
Bargains while they last.

What Matters

All night Awake Nausea Headache Feet throbbing
Struggling with despair Imagining What I could take
What I could eat What I could do

I thought about heating pads Electrolytes Hot baths
I lay there considering All the possibilities
All the desperate Possible Impossibilities
All that had happened Hadn't happened
Yesterday Last week Last month My entire life

I wanted to go on vacation Maybe just pack my suitcase
Longed for my old life A new life A total makeover
Decided I'd settle For a day at the spa Yearned
For my daughter's company The kind voice Of a friend

I thought about my days Consumed by illness
Crammed full Of medical regimen Doctor appointments
Immune globulin infusions Insurance fights

I wanted more chances More choices More health
More time I turned over in bed Hoped lying on the other side
Would change My perspective

I tried to console myself Imagine A different reality
Imagined my feet On the path I used to hike in the woods
Envisioned fresh air Damp woods My body
Navigating the slopes

I wanted to walk in the snow Feel the cold on my skin
My sinuses contract Mouth and fingers Numb
I wanted to scream Howl Do anything But lie in pain
Ruminating Silently Invisibly Grieving

Could I have done anything differently? Avoided this fate?
Could I have made other choices That would have landed me
Somewhere other Than where I was Now?

I realized   I had lived through decades   Countless nights
Of utter despair   Appreciated   The sun would come up
Knew   I had a long list   Of things to do   Call the pharmacy
Reschedule the dermatologist   Do two loads of laundry
Finish the taxes   Fix the broken toilet

I decided   What I had   Wasn't   What I wanted
Wasn't   What I deserved   Realized   It could be worse

In the wee hours   Of the morning   I settled for gratitude
The warm house   Working refrigerator
Brain   That still works   Heart   Still open   Soul
Which still hopes   And wants   Schemes   And plans

Knowing that   Even with illness   And isolation   My one life
Matters   My unpublished poems   Still important
My one small voice   One small life   Worthy enough
To power through   Another day

The Iris

I didn't want to throw out
the purple iris, wilting on the table.
Is it any less beautiful in its withering
state? Entropy surrounds us, both
in our late sixties: old house, frayed rug
at the kitchen sink, old boots, flannel
shirt, thread-bare at collar and cuffs.
Will anyone notice past the gray hair,
fallen mouth and double chin, that I
have a new hairstyle, am wearing
skinny jeans? I decided to keep the iris
hospiced on the table. Celebrated
its aging beauty with tea and toast.

About the Author

Marilyn McVicker had her first poem published in 1980. Her poetry has been most recently published in *Kakalak, Kaleidoscope, The Healing Muse, Earth's Daughters, Front Porch Review, Red Clay Review, Speckled Trout Review, Wordgathering, Breath & Shadow*, and *Red Headed Stepchild*. Her non-fiction book, *Sauna Detoxification Therapy*, was published by McFarland & Co., in 1997, and her poetry chapbook, *Some Shimmer of You*, by Finishing Line Press, in 2014. In 2020, she received an Honorable Mention for her full-length poetry manuscript, *As for Life*, through North Carolina Poetry Society's Lena M. Shull Book Contest. She has read her poetry at numerous festivals, bookstores, colleges, libraries, and other venues. Marilyn's fascination with words and self-expression stems from her previous career as a solo flutist and music educator. She retired to a remote cove in the rural mountains of western North Carolina in 1997.

www.ingramcontent.com/pod-product-compliance
Lightning Source LLC
Chambersburg PA
CBHW071138090426
42736CB00012B/2159